God is the Truth

Michael John DeNucci

Cover photo credit: Michael John DeNucci

Michael John DeNucci
Cumberland, WI

Second Edition
February 2024
Printed in the United States
By http://thebookpatch.com
ISBN: 9798890903372

First Edition June 20, 2022

Acknowledgements

First and foremost, I thank God, Who, through the Holy Spirit, inspired me to write this book. My gratitude to God is overwhelming!

Also, I thank my siblings and friends for supporting me in writing this book. In particular, I thank my brother Donald for facilitating the editing and publishing of this book.

Table of Contents

Preface

God is Love. Love is the Truth. God is Happiness.
Happiness is the Truth. The Truth shall set you Free.
Therefore, God is Freedom and the Truth.

Introduction

"Lord, make me an instrument of your Love, Peace and
Inspiration". This quote is from article 97, "My Prayer",
in my book "Is God Happiness?" I believe that God has
answered my prayer by making me that instrument. It
is my hope that God's message as promoted in my
books will help the readers better serve God and
others.

1
From One Who Has Much, Much is Expected

God expects us to use our talents and resources which He and others have given us for His Kingdom by helping others. These talents could be talents of music, speaking, writing or simply other good deeds or material gifts, including money. He expects us to use these talents according to how much we have been given. From one who has much, much is expected.

A story comes to mind of Mother Theresa asking a rich man for a financial contribution to help the poor. He offered one million dollars. She replied that that was not enough, for she must have known how wealthy the man was.

Finally, if we do not receive a thank you from others after giving these gifts, God always thanks us and will bless us in some way, either in this lifetime or the next, or both. God never cheats us. God is the Truth!

2
The Holy Spirit: The Truth

The Holy Spirit is a real person, not just a concept or belief. He is the third person in the Blessed Trinity. He can guide us through the Bible or other religious readings or other persons to know the Truth.

We should always open our minds, hearts and souls to know the Truth through the Holy Spirit, instead of being trapped by prejudice or ignorance. God is the Truth!

3
My Writings: Like Taking an Essay Test for God

When I write, I let thoughts come to me, which I believe are the truth to promote virtue. I think if I do this in a most understandable way for readers, God grades me with an A+. I do realize that my writings are not perfect, but do my best, which is all that God expects.

God expects all of us to use our talents and many of us do just that. But we all have different talents, so there is NO "one size fits so all". Each of us has talents "tailored" to our very being— our souls. God always thanks us for using our talents, and if we use them wisely to promote virtue based on the Truth, God will give us an A+. God is the Truth!

4
Do We Sometimes Forget the "Big Picture"?

At times, I have found that I get so "bogged down" with details that I forget the "big picture". What is it I really want to accomplish with my activity?

Do we keep the goal of virtue leading us to Heaven in mind? Do we keep God and the Truth in mind? The Truth from God is of ultimate importance. God is the Truth!

5
Enjoying the "Fruits of Our Labor"

I just woke up from a nap refreshed and ready to continue my work for the day. I had just begun typing my manuscript into the I pad for my book: "Is God Freedom?" So, I felt that I deserved my nap as a break and reward from that work.

We should enjoy our achievements and not feel guilty or unworthy of the Joy that they give us. If God appreciates our achievements, why shouldn't we?

I have enjoyed the satisfaction from writing my books, knowing that I can share them with others, who can share them with others, also. I have written what I believe to be the Truth, philosophically and theologically. God is the Truth!

6
Is the Road to Hell "Paved" with Good Intentions?

No! I do NOT believe that the road to hell is paved with truly good intentions. Truly good intentions may result in sacrifice, but God rewards us for such sacrifice. Truly good intentions, when acted upon, are always rewarded by God, if not by others.

The road to hell is paved by selfish intentions that we hope to benefits only ourselves, not God or others. Such selfishness leads to suffering for the selfish one and possibly others. We jeopardize our relationship with God when we act on selfish desires, and I believe we cannot be truly happy without that relationship.

Virtue is acting on truly good intentions and leads to everlasting happiness—ultimately Heaven. God is Love, Happiness, Freedom and the Truth!

7
God's Path for Us

A good friend of mine once said that we do not know God's path or plan for us until the plan unfolds. Consider the Desiderata poem written by Max Ehrmann in 1927: "the universe is unfolding as it should". It is doing so because it is God's plan to do so.

8
Prayer to Your Guardian Angel

"Angel of God, my guardian dear, to whom God's love commits me here, ever this day be at my side, to light, to guard, to rule and guide. Amen." (From Companion Prayers, page 37)

The above is a prayer I learned as a child. We should always remember that God has a guardian angel watching over us and remember to thank that angel for his/her protection and guidance.

9
Should We ever Take a Vacation from Spirituality?

NO! Spirituality is our attempt to be Holy or Godlike. Satan is eager to have us take such a vacation, so the he can tempt us to sin.

To maintain freedom from sin, we must continue our struggle against Satan and move towards virtue and God. We must strive for this Spiritual Perfection which we will probably not completely achieve in this lifetime.

Padre Pio, a Catholic Saint, experienced such a struggle, and I surmise that it might have been Satan, not God, who gave him the stigmata—the wounds of Christ on his body. He may have done this to harm St. Padre Pio, who was doing so much good—listening to other's confessions for long hours and offering his advice. But I think the stigmata only increased his resolve to work towards Spiritual perfection.

Finally, in "Through the Year with Padre Pio" p. 112 by Patricia Treece, she quotes from the Bible: "Beloved, do not believe every spirit, but test the spirits to see whether they are of God". 1 John 4:1 Padre Pio reportedly had visions, both from evil demons and from angels, but remained faithful to God. St. Padre Pio implied that to "take a vacation from Spirituality" is to invite Satan with his punishment and temptations. His life was so remarkable that he was Canonized as a Twentieth Century Saint by the Catholic Church, after living a full and good life as a Catholic Priest.

The following is an excerpt from "Through the Year with Padre Pio" by Patricia Treece, p.37-38:

"Therefore, we must be patient when getting rid of bad habits, dominating aversions and overcoming our own inclinations and humor, when necessary, because this life is a continual struggle and nobody can say: "I am not assailed". Calm is reserved for heaven. On Earth we must fight amid hope and fear, on condition, however, that hope is always stronger… (because of) the omnipotence of He who comes to our aid."

St. Padre Pio knew that God is the Truth and lived his life accordingly.

10
Is Science a Religion?

Through science and its applications with inventions have come many benefits for Mankind. Our higher standard of living today, compared to the past, is largely due to progress from science.

But, we must remember that what we are discovering to help us was created by and is maintained by God. God created the Universe and it's unfolding or changing. We are simply observers and appliers of this knowledge of the Universe to improve our living conditions. Such work is virtuous if it does so. Scientists, researchers, engineers, inventors, medical persons and all involved in these virtuous applications of science deserve our acknowledgment and a thank you.

However, to believe that science today has all the answers to our questions in life is incorrect. There is still so much we do not understand about the material world. It still holds mysteries.

Finally, science has laws to follow to gain knowledge and laws gained from knowledge. Religion is "how we relate" to God, which also has laws. All knowledge and its virtuous applications come, ultimately, from God. Science is not a religion, but gives us the tools to improve our lives and even our religion by knowing more about God's creation and how to use such knowledge. God is the Truth!

11
Do We Communicate What We Feel or What We Believe?

Communication is an important activity. It can be telling others what we think and believe. This, of course can include how we "feel" about issues or topics.

However, we should want to present to others what we truly think and believe, not necessarily what we "feel". What we "feel" may be temporary and misleading concerning what our convictions are—what we believe. "Gut level feelings" might be accurate, but we should examine them to discern whether they are really what we believe to be true. Instead of going with unexamined "gut level feelings", we should consider how such "feelings" will be interpreted by others. Communication is an important activity, so we should present ourselves as who we really are rather than what we "feel" without really thinking it over.

This is not to say that we should be cold and calculating, but that we should not misrepresent our true selves, but tell people what we truly think and believe. If we believe in God, that should be reflected in our communication, not just emotionally, but carefully and logically.

Let's present what we "believe" is the truth. God is the Truth!

12
Could Our Personal Morality Affect Others?

When we think of morality, we usually think of what is personally right or wrong to us. However, our personal morality can and often does affect others. What we say and do often does affect others.

We have a moral responsibility to consider those effects. Let's keep our words and deeds virtuous, thinking of others, not just ourselves. This follows from the Commandment of Jesus: Love Our Neighbor as Ourselves. God is the Truth!

13
Overconfidence

Sometimes, some of us, including myself, have been overconfident— "cock sure". We feel so sure of ourselves that we are not aware of the dangers around us. We are presumptuous.

Such overconfidence shows that we lack humility—the humility to realize that we may not know everything about the situation we are in. From humility, we can realize our limitations and turn to God for a healthy confidence based on our confidence in Him. We can be sure that our faith in Him is the Truth. God is the Truth!

14
"When I am Weak, then I am Strong"

St. Paul said not to boast about ourselves, "except about our weaknesses". Cor 12:5. "Therefore, I am content with weaknesses, insults, hardships, persecutions, and constraints, for the sake of Christ, for when I am weak, then I am strong." Cor12:10. Humility requires that we accept the "crosses to bear" in our lives for Christ's sake and do not take full credit for our achievements, but recognize that they are due, not only to our own efforts, but also due to Divine assistance and assistance from others. Pride can ruin the good work done when we take total credit for it ourselves.

If we let the Holy Spirit work through us, we can accomplish great deeds, but more due to the Holy Spirit than ourselves. Humility brings us to know the Truth. God is the Truth!

15
Is There Only One Path to Heaven?

I believe that too many people believe they have the "only" path to heaven. They rule out other Christian denominations and non-Christian religions. How can anyone say that he/she has the only path to Heaven? Only God can determine that.

If we believe that the soul is eternal, which is proposed by many contemporary theologians, then the soul lives on after earthly death. Why deny that others can enter Heaven just because they do not share our beliefs?

Goodness is not reserved for any particular religion or denomination of any religion. We should not discount people who disagree with our religious doctrines, but keep an open mind to follow Jesus: Love God with All Your Heart, Mind, Soul and Strength, and Love Your Neighbor as Yourself. We cannot judge whether people love God and others, and should give them the benefit of the doubt by loving them.

In conclusion, we should not wish to condemn anyone to hell, because that is judgmental, which Jesus warned against. God is Love. If people practice Love, certainly God will smile on them for doing so and may even reward them in some way, even in the afterlife, for living a "good" life. God is the Truth!

16
Nobody is Promised Tomorrow

We make plans for the future—tomorrow—often assuming that tomorrow will come. However, we should consider the reading in Scripture of the wealthy man who had a plentiful harvest, so he decided to build more barns to hold his "bumper crops", and then, just "kick back" to enjoy the fruits of his labors.

However, that man died that very night, so he could not enjoy the "fruits of his labors". The lesson is that we must to ready to die at any time. No one is promised tomorrow.

In conclusion, we should certainly prepare for the future, even if it means enjoying the fruits of our labor.

But, we must always realize that God could call us at any time. He has the final say in whether our plans are fulfilled or not. God is the Truth!

17
Do We Sometimes "Stumble" on Our Way to Heaven?

Sometimes, we may have trouble staying on the "straight and narrow path" in life. We may "stumble" and "weave off course". At times like these, God does not abandon us, but offers us hope to get back on the path of righteousness. This righteousness should mean righteous in the "eyes of God", not just righteous in "our own eyes", which is "self-righteousness", and is based on pride.

By maintaining a healthy humility, we can admit our "stumbling" to God, so that we can get back on track on the road to heaven. If we need forgiveness, we can ask for it and reconcile with God, Who is the Truth!

18
Do We Owe a Debt to God after Sinning?

I do not think of our relationship with God as a "business relationship". God does NOT require us to "pay a debt to Him" after sinning. We simply need to admit guilt, express remorse and ask for forgiveness, which He will grant us FREELY, because He misses us and wants us back—just as a good friend would.

God is not a businessman trying to increase His profit, but I believe He has a human trait of a NEED for our love in a spiritual relationship. Let's give our love to God because we want to give Him the GIFT of our love, rather than paying a debt to Him for sinning. This Truth is exemplified by Jesus Christ, Who is the Way, the Truth and the Life!

19
Do We "Dig Down Deep" to Help Others?

I just woke up from a nap with the mental picture of my reaching to the bottom of my big barrel, which had been filled with pop and beer cans to crush for recycling.

I drew the comparison to others who need our help. Do we reach down deep into society's disadvantaged people to help them materially or even Spiritually? Or, are we "snobbish", thinking we are too good to help them because we consider them "below us"? So, we deny others the help that they need.

Jesus said: "Love your neighbor as yourself, and do unto others what you would have them do unto you." A snob is selfish and does not respect and love everyone. Let's practice LOVE and NOT snobbery. Just as God is Love, so we can be Love by obeying His commandments to Love.

20
Spiritual Progress

I believe that Spiritual Progress is the result of striving for perfection of our spirits or our souls. We do this by practicing love rather than revenge.

Jesus taught us that we should forget justice based on revenge— "an eye for an eye and a tooth for a tooth".

Instead, He offered the commandments of Love of God and Love of Our Neighbor as ourselves. By doing so we achieve Spiritual progress. This Spiritual progress can be attained by anyone who practices Love according to the teachings of Jesus Christ!

21
Do We have Regrets?

Some of us have regrets in our lives. Regrets serve a purpose—to promise to God and others, if possible, and to ourselves that we will avoid making those mistakes again.

I have no regrets for what God has done for me. Divine Providence certainly proved to me that God cares about me by granting me protection and favors, which increased my love and gratitude to Him. Also, I thank others who have helped me.

Scriptures says: "Know the Truth and the Truth will set you free". John 8:32. Also, "He who is without love does not know God, for God is Love". 1 John 4:7-8 and my book God is Love, Preface. So to know God is to know Love. Jesus said He was the Truth. So, to know God is to know Love, Freedom and the Truth!

22
"If We Do Not Have Love, We are Nothing"

"If I speak in human and angelic tongues, but do not have love, I am a resounding gong or clashing cymbal. And if I have the gift of prophecy and comprehend all mysteries and all knowledge, if I have all faith so as to move mountains, but do not have love, I am nothing. If I give away everything I own and if I hand my body over so that I may boast, but do not have love, I gain nothing…So faith, hope and love remain, these three, but the greatest of these is love." 1 Corinthians; 13:1-3,13 and "All That Matters is Love "(article 78, my book: "God is Love")

23
What is Wisdom?

Funk and Wagnalls dictionary defines wisdom as: "The power of true and right discernment"; also, "the conformity to the course of action by such discernment".

The pursuit for Wisdom can involve the "discernment" of Spirits. Spirits can be in the form of thoughts, or even "voices" or "apparitions", which St. Padre Pio reputedly experienced. Such Spirits can be either Good or bad—inspiring one to do something virtuous or tempting one to commit evil or sin, or at times can cause painful attacks of physical, mental or emotional suffering when none is warranted. Evil Spirits can cause such suffering because their victim, like St. Padre Pio, who received the wounds of Christ, is their enemy because such person works for virtue and despises sin and evil spirits.

Wisdom facilitates the "discernment" to know whether the Spirits are good or bad. From wisdom comes good, sound decisions on which to base virtuous actions. Wisdom is the first gift of the Holy Spirit. (Isaiah 11:1-3). The Holy Spirit is the third person in the Blessed Trinity or God. God is the Truth!

24
Is Hate or Fear the Opposite of Love?

I believe that fear is a barrier to Love, but not Love's opposite. Fear works to prevent love to try to protect ourselves.

However, hate is a conscious decision completely disregarding Love which often results in willingly wanting harm to others. Hate is the opposite of Love, unlike fear which is a "weakness" which can prevent Love.

Virtue is free of hate. However, virtue does not abolish fear unless it includes Faith and Trust in God to overcome the fear. By trusting God, we will not hate or fear. God is the Love, Freedom and the Truth!

25
Are We Patient with Ourselves and Others?

At times, I have found that I was not patient with myself and /or others. If I saw a need to do something, I sometimes thought that it had to be done "right now".

However, we are all limited in our abilities or talents and "time". Sometimes, we may not be "ready" to perform some task or do not have time to do it. We should be patient with ourselves to "put something off" until we are ready and have time to do so.

At times I have found that I was impatient concerning my writings or receiving my completed books. I know now that I have the "right to put off" work on my books until I am truly ready to do it.

Likewise, we should be patient with others and realize that they too are limited in their time and talent.

If we are patient with ourselves and others, we will do what God expects of us at the proper time. God is the Truth!

26
Slowing Down

Since retiring from the US Postal Service about 18 years ago, I have found that my habit of doing everything as fast as I could still remains with me. I considered "speed" an obligation in that job and others jobs I had before that. So, yet today, I hurry when I eat, I hurry when I do manual labor and I hurry when am on errands. I have found it very difficult for me to "slow down", though I do not work for any earthly organization anymore.

People have told me to "slow down". Some have said that I looked like I was "on a mission". I once encountered a resident of the local congregate housing, connected to the Nursing Home, who described my hurrying that way. I replied with the words of the song "I am in a Hurry" by the group Alabama written by Roger Murray and Randy Van Warmer: "I am in a hurry to get things done. Oh, I rush and rush until life's no fun…. All I really got to do is live and die, but I'm in a hurry and don't know why".

This "rushing around" is probably pent-up anxiety, but like the song, I really don't know why I am in a hurry. Perhaps, it is a carryover from work requiring speed much of my life.

However, with me and others, I believe that if we don't "slow down" and "smell the roses", we jeopardize our physical and mental health as well as our Happiness. As God is Happiness and the Truth, we should turn to Him to give us direction in our lives to help us "slow down", if we believe we should "slow down".

27
Is Our Love Meant to Share with People or Only with God?

With relative isolation during the Covid pandemic, some of us, including me, decided not to share our love with others "in person", but only on phones or other media, out of health precautions. But, God was open to our Love during this period.

We have a need for socialization—a need for sharing our Love with others. True, God is the source of all Love, but we should try to share Love with others as much as we can. The second commandment of Jesus: "Love your neighbor as yourself" commands us to do so.

Isolation due to the pandemic brought many of us to realize how important is our sharing love with others. Then, when we feel comfortable to be with them "in person", we can appreciate such "sharing" more than before the pandemic.

Just as God deserves our Love, so do others deserve our love. God is Love and the Truth!

28
Is God's Love Unconditional?

God loves us just as we are. We don't need to prove that we are worthy of His Love by our performance.

(My book "God is Love", article 37, and Catholic Herald by Fr. Mike Schmitz, p.13, July 23, 2020)

Jesus proved His Love to us with His passion, death and Resurrection. His Love for us is unconditional. God always loves us and offers us repentance from sin, if necessary, as He is Happiness and the Truth!

29
"To Know Him is to Love Him"

The above title is the title of a song by the Teddy Bears and written by Phil Spector from 1959. I propose the analogy that to know God is to love Him, for God is Love. He who knows God knows Love.

"Everyone who Loves is begotten by God and knows God. Whoever is without Love does not know God, for God is Love." 1 John 4:7-8

30
Should We be Pragmatic?

Pragmatism is defined in Funk and Wagnalls dictionary as: "the doctrine that ideas have value only in terms of their practical consequences, and that results are the sole test of validity or truth of one's belief". Let's look at pragmatism concerning Christ's passion, death and Resurrection. One may say Christ's life appears to have ended in disaster with His crucifixion, so He did not live "pragmatically".

However, if we believe in His Resurrection from the dead, we know that His life was justified. Thus, Jesus was "pragmatic" in what He did, though it did not appear so until His Resurrection.

Pragmatism is based on proven success of our actions. However, like Jesus, our success may not necessarily be measured in this lifetime, but in eternity. Thus, what may look like failure in this lifetime may actually be ultimate success in terms of eternity. Just as Jesus was the Truth and proved it "pragmatically" by His Resurrection, so we can prove our success in eternity by practicing love of God and others, inheriting His

promised everlasting Life and Happiness in Heaven.
God is the Truth!

31
Does God Inspire Music?

Yes! I believe that God does inspire some music
through the Holy Spirit, particularly songs with a
religious message and songs of love.

What comes to mind for me are the songs "Who Will
Answer?" written by Phil Spector and Shiela Davis and
"My Cup Runnith Over" written by Harvey Schmidt and
Tom Jones for the musical "I Do, I Do".

Both songs are were sung by Ed Ames. Listen to them
sometime if you are not familiar with them and can do
so.

I believe that the Holy Spirit inspires songwriters to
write both the lyrics and melodies of such songs.
Then, He inspires singers and musicians to perform
them.

Music is very important to me, as I have a "library" of
thousands of songs which I have chosen from
YouTube for my I Pad and Phone. I can listen to any of

them almost anytime I desire. Music has been a blessing to me and I thank God for that blessing which gives me much happiness. God is Love, Happiness, Freedom and the Truth!

32
What Does Patriotism Mean?

Patriotism is love for one's country or nation. Love is wishing well and doing good unto others, as much as we can.

Patriotism is love if it means loving one's country to promote and practice love by offering benefits to its citizens, and to other nations "foreign aid" or some other benefit, such as their defense against hostile enemies.

However, if love of country leads to conquering another nation for benefit of only the conquering nation without considering the welfare of the conquered nation, that is not Love, and, therefore, not true patriotism. Such aggression toward nations is based on "greed". Only by practicing Love for the sake of Justice can world peace be attained and maintained. Just as Love is Freedom and the Truth, so God is Freedom and the Truth!

33
Go for the Ride with Jesus as Your Guide

Heaven is promised to those who follow Christ's two commandments of Love: Love God above all and Love your neighbor as yourself. Let Jesus be your guide. (See my book: Fishing for Heaven.)

So, if your go for the "ride" with Jesus as your conductor/pilot/guide you will reach your destination— Heaven!

However, it may be a "bumpy ride". One may have to suffer for practicing some beliefs or simply expressing them. Jesus said that you must "take up your cross" if you follow Him. Some Saints have encountered persecution due to practicing or expressing their beliefs in Jesus. Some have even succumbed to martyrdom for doing so. The Catholic Church has canonized some of them as Saints. Thus, they are venerated by the living and loved by God and all the Saints and Angels in Heaven.

It may be a bumpy road to heaven, but our destination will be secure if we follow Jesus. He is the Way, the Truth and the Life. God is the Truth!

34
What are Social Needs?

We all have some social needs—the needs to be in the company of others to give and receive attention to and from them. This can be in the physical company of others or through some media. We grew up with such needs in our families.

However, as we grew older, we tended to choose those who would be in our company to satisfy those needs rather than being limited to our families. Maslow included "love" as a human need above basic physical needs. This need involves human contact.

Some of us have experienced a reduction in physical social contact due to the Covid pandemic. But, social needs are relative, not absolute. Each of us has different social needs. There is no "one size fits all".

In conclusion, even Christ recognized social needs which resulted in social justice required by His

Commandment of Love of Neighbor as Ourselves. By loving others, we achieve the social need of "giving love". If we receive love in return, that is a bonus which can give us "enhanced" happiness. As God is Happiness and Freedom, God is the Truth!

35
Are We Just "Taking Care of Business"?

At times I am motivated to "take care of business": pay the bills, mail letters, shop for groceries or other things, and clean the house. Accomplishing such tasks give me satisfaction.

However, does such satisfaction lead to happiness? When completed, it is more of a "relief" than a positive move giving me happiness. To find happiness, I turn to music and conversations with others, even if only through the media—text messages, emails— or actual vocal talks on the phone. Listening to music, I find lifts my spirits. After doing such things, I am sometimes motivated to do something creative, like writing for my books, which can give me ecstasy rather than just the relief gained from accomplishing mundane tasks.

If we can, use our creativity we can achieve Maslow's highest need: self-actualization—achieving our highest potential. It is very satisfying, even to the point of ecstasy, to do so.

But, each of us has a different way of being creative and should find our own way. There is no "one size fits all".

None of this is to say that we should not take care of mundane matters. "Take care of business", but we should consider that this is only the "beginning". If we let the Holy Spirit work within us, we may "rise above mundane matters" and express ourselves virtuously and creatively. I believe that God is pleased when we do so. God is the Truth!

36
Do We React to Only Those with a "Voice"?

We have paid attention to those who have protested and even caused destruction in our society (i.e., after the death of George Floyd). However, those innocent babies destroyed by abortion have no "voice". They are not heard by anyone, certainly not those responsible for the abortions or the laws and some persons interpreting the laws that allow them.

It is not so evident that abortion is killing human life as much as killing a human born and already outside the womb. But, that does not make their lives any less valuable. An aborted human may have had the potential to have been a big asset to God and humanity. Who are we to decide that a human life within the womb should end?

After science determines that human life has begun in the womb, it should be protected by laws just as those outside the womb are protected by laws. A woman does NOT have the right to kill her baby, even if it is still in the womb and not completely developed. Human life is SACRED and God demands that we protect it. God is the Truth!

37
Under Stress, Do We Do What We Really Want to Do?

Under stress we may feel compelled to do or say something that we really do not want to do or say. We may feel that we do not have time to think it over.

It is best that we do NOT allow ourselves to be in such a position of stress. We do have limited patience. However, we sometimes find it difficult to avoid such stressful situations.

I have succumbed to unwanted results of my behavior due to stress. If we have offended others in such situations, we should always apologize and ask for forgiveness from them, if possible. Also, we should ask forgiveness from God if we have offended Him.

Finally, if we find ourselves in such stress, we should pray for patience. It is an important virtue. We should practice the commandment of Jesus to Love one another. God is the Truth!

38
Do We Give Back Love to God?

I have said in my book "Happiness is the Truth", art. 36, that God always reciprocates love back to us when we express love to Him.

However, it is God who loves us first, before we are even capable of giving love, until we learn it as children. We should always remember to give Love back to God. His Love is infinite and unconditional, unlike ours which is limited. However, we can Love God with all our Heart, Mind, Soul and Strength as commanded by Jesus.

39
Do We "Salute" God?

In the military, servicemen come to "attention" and salute their officers. Also, servicemen come to attention and salute the American Flag.

But, do we give God "attention" by figuratively "saluting" Him out of respect through worship and prayer. The first Commandment of Jesus requires that we "give all our Love" when giving attention to God. This may include music and prayer when worshiping Him. God certainly is due our attention, for He is the Truth!

40
"The Impossible Dream"

"To bear with unbearable sorrow; to run where the brave dare not go; to right the unrightable wrong…To be willing to march into hell for that Heavenly cause…To dream the impossible dream."

The above are words to the song "The Impossible Dream" sung "by Steve Lawrence and others and written by Tom Darion. It could fit the mission of Jesus Christ, Who actually DID achieve the "impossible"— Resurrection from the dead. He promised the "impossible" for us too—Everlasting Life! So, just as Jesus could obtain the "impossible dream", so can we if we follow Him to achieve it. God is the Truth!

41
Confession: God Loves Us

A while ago, I confessed my sins to a priest. After doing so, the priest said: "Remember, God loves you". That statement was and still is very important to me. God always loves us, even when we sin. He never rejects us and we should never reject Him. After hearing these words from the priest and receiving his formal absolution, my soul was again at peace, knowing that God loved me enough to forgive me.

Even the most serious sins can be forgiven if we honestly repent. Such forgiveness gives us Freedom to move forward based on the Truth. God is the Truth!

42
What is Happiness?

Couldn't Happiness be listening to a favorite song? Isn't Happiness simply Serenity and inner Peace? Isn't it the absence of worry? If we trust God with our future, we will attain Happiness with Serenity and Peace. This peace must include Peace with others. Love of God and others is the life force that brings us Serenity, Peace, and Happiness.

If we do have problems, God can help us solve those problems to attain Serenity. Consider the Serenity Prayer written by Reinhold Niebuhr: "God grant me the Serenity to accept what cannot be changed, the courage to change what can be changed and the wisdom to know one from the other".

However, Happiness is not "complacency". We should not be satisfied with mediocre Spiritual Health, but attempt to gain more Spiritual Growth through helping others out of Love for them and for God. From such Love comes Happiness and Freedom based on the Truth. God is the Truth.

43
Is Religion a Science?

Some contemporary "theologians" appear to me to try to make religion into some sort of "science". One theory is that God is "pure energy" and that we become "pure energy" in the afterlife. This theory has some basis in science, which I am not qualified to address.

Religion is defined as "how we relate to God". If we lose our "personal" and "human" way of relating to God, we might lose "religion" to substitute "science" in its place. Some of these contemporary "theologians" might believe that they have discovered something new. I am not qualified to completely understand the science behind their "theory', but it is just an "unproven theory", not a fact.

Personally, I find it more meaningful and rewarding to relate to God on a "personal" and "human" level.

In conclusion, religion is not a "science", but requires Faith to believe in God, Whom we do not fully understand. The Holy Bible can give us insights into Who God is, especially through Jesus Christ. Also, we can gain insights into God by belief in the Blessed Trinity, which is a mystery. God is the Truth!

44
Does God Love Us even if He is "Pure Energy"?

Many of us think of God as a person, like ourselves. We may think of Him in a human fashion. However, some contemporary theologians think of God as "pure energy".

Even if God is "pure energy", I believe He still has intelligence and can know us in a human way. Why limit God by saying He cannot know us that way? Our knowledge of God is limited, but we can learn about Him from the Bible, religious readings, other persons and life experiences. In particular, can learn about God from the teachings and example of Jesus Christ.

It has not been proven that God is "pure energy". It all comes down to "what we believe". If we believe in God in a way that helps us "relate to Him" and is based on what we believe to be the truth about Him, I believe that approach is valid. To me, God is still the subject of religion, not so much the subject of science. God is the Truth!

45
Timing Again in My Life

As I was just now reading "Timing in My Life", article 6 of my book "God is Freedom?", the song "Good Timin" sung by Jimmy Jones and written by Fred Tobias and Clint Ballard, Jr. played on my I Pad. I did NOT plan that. It just happened. God leads me "every inch of the way". God is the Truth!

46
Is Doing Nothing Ever an Option?

Sometimes when facing a difficult situation, we might not know what to do. Some people might say: "Do something, even if it is wrong". I do not agree with that statement. Never intentionally do something if we believe it is wrong. Doing nothing is better than doing something wrong. Sin is NEVER the answer, though it may seem expedient to commit the sin to get results.

In conclusion, I believe that if we do not know which path to take in a difficult situation, we should pause to pray for guidance and reflect on our life experiences. We may find when we do this, we will gain wisdom to make the right decision, based on the Truth. God is the Truth!

47
Do Love and Forgiveness Always Include Trust?

We can love and forgive someone who has offended us without trusting them. Love and forgiveness go "hand in hand".

However, trust is different. It usually must be earned. (See my books: "Thoughts and Writings", article 42 and "God is Love", article 2.). If the risk to trust someone, based on their past behavior, outweighs the possible benefits of trusting them, we should probably not trust them.

However, sometimes we take a "leap of faith" and trust someone if much is likely to be gained from trusting them. This does occur in dating and marital relationships, and sometimes even in friendships.

We can always trust God, and through that trust we can gain wisdom to know whether or not to trust others. God is the Truth!

48
Can There be Spirituality without Religion?

Spirituality refers to the life of the spirit or soul. Religion is "relating to God". I do not believe that we can have Spirituality, in terms of striving for spiritual growth, without Religion. Indeed, how can our souls be "alive" without "relating to God"?

However, I do NOT believe that a person needs to belong to, or practice, any organized religion to be religious or spiritual. But, organized religions have given us "order" or "structure" to follow in our relationships to God in our attempts at Spirituality. Without some "order", this relationship to God is very difficult, if not impossible. Organized religion has certainly done much to improve our relationships with God and the resulting Spirituality.

Thus, Religion is necessary for Spirituality. It is the means by which we attain it. Through Religion we learn that God is the Truth!

49
Experiencing Beauty in Life

I just woke up from a nap to hear the beautiful song: "Love Me With All of Your Heart" playing on my I Pad. I realize that life would not be as enjoyable without beauty in nature, music, art or some other form, including the physical beauty of humans. This beauty can present Love as in a song like the one I am now listening to.

Without beauty in our world as an expression of Love in some way, I think life would be boring and drab. Music brings much beauty into my life. Another song is now playing on my I Pad as I write: "Love Put a Song in My Heart" by Johnny Rodrigues and written by Ben Peters. All beauty, ultimately, come from God—its creator. God is Love, Happiness, Freedom, Truth and Beauty!

50
Love and Inspiration, Not Judgment and Condemnation

I know that I have repeatedly addressed Love and Inspiration in my books. But, I cannot stress enough how important they are in our lives, physically, emotionally and spiritually.

Let's take a "positive" view of God and others as much as we can. Love and Inspiration can accomplish so much more than judgment and condemnation. Like Jesus, try to SAVE the world rather than condemn it. Thus, if we realize that God is the Truth, He can help us make a difference in our own lives and the lives of others.

God Love and Bless You!

Michael John DeNucci lives in Cumberland, WI and is a freelance writer for God and Mankind

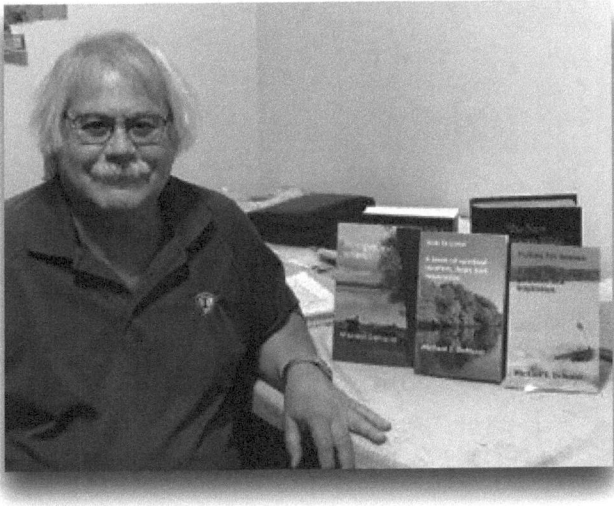

Michael John DeNucci attended his first two years of high school at Holy Cross Seminary in Lacrosse, Wisconsin and then returned to graduate from Cumberland High School. He went on to earn his Bachelor's Degree in Political Science from the College of St Thomas in St Paul, Minnesota, attended the University of Wisconsin at Madison partially completing an MBA, and then earning a Master's Degree in Industrial Relations from the University of Minnesota. He is an Army Veteran who has served stateside and in Germany. He has held a variety of jobs over his lifetime which have broadened his perspectives on the relationship of God and Mankind.

Other Books by Michael John DeNucci

"Thoughts and Writings"

"Fishing for Heaven"

"God is Love"

"Is God Happiness"

"Is Love the Truth"

"Happiness is the Truth"

"Is God Freedom?"

"Is Love Freedom"

"Is God Mercy"

"Is God Peace?"

◀